◇◇◇◇◇◇◇◇◇◇◇◇◇◇◇◇◇◇

Cover Design
and
YOU!

Dos, Don'ts, & Choices

By

Annie Acorn
&
Angel Nichols

Table of Contents

Cover Design & YOU!

Introduction

Traditional vs. Indie, on whichever side of the argument they fall or even if they span the two, every author will, at some point, find themselves in the position of relying on a cover artist to aid in the promotion of their work.

Gone are the days when artists, such as Tom Adams, painted the covers that graced the novels of such notables as Agatha Christie and Raymond Chandler. The computer age dawned long ago, and graphic designers now rule.

Still, the choices facing an author or boutique publisher are many, and they are topped only by the number of pitfalls that face the unwary.

Feeling fortunate in the success of our working relationship that now spans four years, we determined to write this book as authors, a publisher, and a graphic designer.

Our hope is that, by sharing our knowledge, expertise and experiences, we may smooth the paths of others who are working hard to make their literary dreams come true.

Angel Nichols – author and graphic designer
Annie Acorn – author and boutique publisher

How It Started

Annie Acorn -

One day, I woke up in desperate need of a cover designer – not a regular occurrence in anyone's life. It all started like this:

Many years ago now, I was lunching with a friend – Andre Arnett of New Breed Marketer.

"Don't you write?" he asked.

"All the time," I answered. "I have drawers full of stuff in my office at home."

"Then you're sitting on a gold mine," he replied. "I'm fascinated by eMarketing. I know all about websites and blogposts, but I couldn't write a novel or a short story if my life depended on it."

Understanding the meaning of the word 'gold,' I filed this away somewhere deep in my brain, where it took root.

By 2011, frustrated by the confines of traditional publishing, I found myself again at a lunch table with my friend.

"I've been thinking about what you said," I told him.

"That this cheeseburger is good?"

"No, that I'm sitting on a gold mine by not publishing my own work and drawing on your eMarketing experience," I replied.

"It's about time you saw the light." He took a bite of a French fry, chewed, and swallowed. "Why don't I stop by Saturday afternoon and get you started?"

Saturday arrived right on schedule, and I prepared space at my dining room table for two computers, two coasters, a LARGE bowl of Lindts, some peanut M&Ms just in case, a spiral notebook and a number of pens.

Completely verbal myself, I found the idea of buying a domain name, setting up Twitter and Facebook accounts, and hosting a website rather daunting, but Andre had assured me there was nothing to it.

As we sat down to work, I began taking copious notes so I wouldn't forget what I was learning, but as Andre moved things forward step-by-step, one thing struck me loud and clear as a businesswoman.

I had a friend to help and guide me. What would other completely verbal writers and authors, who wanted to take the publishing road less traveled, do? How would they accomplish their goals and make their dreams come true without breaking the bank?

As the previous owner of several fair-sized businesses, I realized I now held the critical component for a successful start-up – a hole that needed to be filled, if my friend would agree to contract his services when needed.

Besides, hadn't I always wanted to mentor budding writers, and what better vehicle was there for doing so than one's own publishing firm?

On May 28, 2011, *The Magic Sand Dollar*, a faith-based children's book by me, was uploaded as an ebook onto KDP Amazon.

In August, 2011, Annie Acorn Publishing, LLC, became a legal entity in the State of Maryland.

Soon authors from the large network I had developed over the years began approaching me as a publisher, and within a brief period of time, From Womens' Pens, a collaborative group of award-winning, internationally read authors, was formed – a uniting element the fact that all of us were publishing at least some of our work through Annie Acorn Publishing, LLC.

The concept of an annual *Annie Acorn's Christmas Treasury* became a reality on September 26, 2011, drawing on the talents of these remarkable women. Rapidly, the proposed offerings of AAPub, as it is known amongst insiders, grew to include everything from full-length works of fiction to non-fiction finance books.

The initial smaller works we had published had been garnished with basic covers created by myself in a free downloaded version of Gimp. None of them were particularly stellar, but they had served the purpose of allowing AAPub to test its wings.

Now, though, we would be publishing the works of others, and they deserved the best possible publication of their work from start to finish. It was time for me to connect with a graphic designer.

Having dealt with interns in relation to other projects, where we had previously worked, Andre and I discussed the possibility of utilizing a graphic design student from a local community college to fill the role.

Both of us liked the idea of providing a talented individual with the opportunity to build a repertoire of work and a body of references, before they launched themselves upon the open market.

Obviously, such a student would have to be nearing graduation and recommended by their professors. As a first step, I made some initial calls, finally identifying the appropriate parties within the college's structure, who could help us.

Appointments were made, and over a period of weeks, we attended several meetings. Everyone agreed what we proposed would create a win/win situation, and then all forward motion stopped.

Confused, we persisted, but to no avail. Concerns were raised as to whether or not students would have time to work on outside projects, be able to access transportation to our work location, and be covered should an accident happen.

Finally, we gave up. What had sounded like a great idea had died before it had even started. What a shame!

Stymied, I gave some serious thought to my next step. I had never worked with any of the graphic designers in the area where I now lived, and I could think of no one who could recommend one. This, I realized, expanded my options.

Unsure of what I would find, I sent my fingers flying across my computer's keyboard. Several local design firms appeared as a result of my search, but it was obvious that their services, while highly professional, would be more than what we required and not necessarily geared towards the book covers that we needed.

Then I spotted it off to the side – a freelance site that featured graphic designers, and somewhat relieved, I clicked on it.

After reading a brief description of the types of services available, I answered a brief survey that narrowed down the designers who would be presented to me for consideration. As near as I can recall, I requested that the candidates would:

- Speak English,
- Work within the continental United States, and
- Fall within a certain price point.

Six designers – all women – appeared on my screen with short bios. Another click allowed me to view examples of their work as well as references in various forms.

After studying the options presented thoroughly, I knew exactly which one I preferred, but this was a collaborative effort, so I called Andre into my office. Refusing to tell him my choice, I gave him a few minutes to consider as I held my breath.

"This one, without a doubt." He pointed at the one that I wanted, and I exhaled.

Younger than the other four candidates, her training was impeccable, and her example work was amazing.

In addition, she lived at that time only a few miles from Birmingham, Alabama, which meant that I would be in a position to meet with her in person, when I returned there to visit with my eldest son and some of the authors of From Women's Pens.

No surprise to you who actually read the names on the cover of this book, her name was Angel Nichols of Angel Wings Design – to me another sign that we had made the right decision, because she was truly the answer to prayer.

On February 1, 2012, a wonderful cover designed by Angel for my cozy mystery *Chocolate Can Kill* was revealed on Twitter and Facebook. On February 12, the full-length novel launched, and early sales were encouraging.

On April 22, 2012, *Chocolate Can Kill* was ranked #1 in its category and #12 on the entire Barnes and Noble website. Annie Acorn Publishing, LLC, had proven itself capable of producing, launching and marketing a winner in less than a year.

Why the phenomenal success of this, my first published novel, in a relatively large genre?

I give the credit to three things:

- A catchy title,
- A well-written blurb, but most of all to
- Angel's fabulous cover

Our creative partnership continues to this day, and while Angel Wings Design has many clients, 98% of AAPub's covers have been designed by Angel, many of them award-winning. We have no reason or desire to change this.

Working with a graphic designer as an author/publisher is similar in many ways to a marriage. I'm thankful every day that Angel and AAPub have forged a good one.

The keys to our success? Not necessarily in this order:

- Trust,
- Mutual respect,
- Good listening skills,
- Professionalism on both sides,
- Good communication skills,
- An ability to give, take, and compromise,
- An understanding and appreciation for deadlines,
- An aversion to drama on both sides,
- An understanding of each other's processes, and
- Angel Nichols is an extremely nice and patient person.

Unfortunately, I have since learned, I was extremely lucky in my search. One only has to spend a few days on Twitter to discover any number of blog posts outlining horror stories related to similar attempts by other authors and/or boutique publishers.

Not only does the quality of the designers available differ widely, but so do their price lists and the way that they are figured. There are no guarantees in the graphic design world, and often it takes several tries to find a good fit.

Once you connect with a designer with whom you work well, hang onto them. They are a special breed indeed.

Thank you, Angel. You mean the world to all of us affiliated with Annie Acorn Publishing, LLC!

Your Cover's Job

A book cover's purpose is to attract the attention of a possible reader and provide them with some sense of the story or material contained on the pages within the manuscript that it represents.

On the flip side, a book cover's purpose is NOT to restate an author's story or research, although it is permissible and, at times, preferable that it reflect these in some way.

Angel Nichols and Annie Acorn

When the Call Came

I was not a new artist when I met Annie in the latter part of 2011, but I was very new at working as a professional graphic designer for hire. I had graduated in 2009, so I was relatively new on the market, and aside from a few one-and-done contracts, I had never really had any dealings with a major company.

When I answered Annie's initial phone call, I was at another part-time job on my lunch break, and despite the fact that I was content with my place there, being an artist was in my blood and it had always been my dream to make a career of it. Keep in mind, the idea of becoming a published author was far and away from anything I had even thought of as a possibility at that point.

Getting the call was, for lack of a better word, weird.

Annie had emailed me in the earlier part of that week, and her email had been a hair's breadth from being put in my spam folder. I didn't recognize her name, and she was offering a dream job. We all get *those* emails once in a while.

Still, for some reason, I opened it, read it, and decided that I would wait for her call.

When Annie first introduced herself on the phone, she sounded exactly like one of my aunts, and for a moment, I thought it might be a prank. Then Annie explained that she had found my profile on an independent contracting website that I had abandoned almost a year earlier, and from hundreds of artists on that site, she had chosen to offer me a contract.

Almost two hours later, the call ended, and I had my first official job as the cover artist for Annie Acorn. I was nervous, terrified, and overwhelmed, but I also had this feeling that something major had just happened.

That first experience could've been awkward, and there was a lot of potential for things to go wrong.

Annie had just been through some awful dealings with an unprofessional 'professional' artist. I was still incredulous that this well-known publisher had picked my abandoned profile off a site about which I had long since forgotten that showed only examples of work I had done for friends, none of which were book covers.

As an artist, I can tell you that every one of us, well known or otherwise, is almost constantly unsure about whether our art is any good. We have this little voice in our heads that tells us with every stroke of the brush that it's total garbage and we should just stop making art for everyone's sake.

I suppose this comes with the territory of being an artist or anything else creative for that matter, including writing, and it's never more true than when creating someone else's vision.

An illustrator is not just another type of artist. An illustrator's job is to take the vision in another person's head and make it come to life on paper, so we have to be part artist, part negotiator, and part psychic. To complicate things, sometimes clients have a hard time putting their vision into words, and other times they are too specific. See what I mean?

- It's a horse, but it's not a horse, you know?
- It's the magical embodiment of Mother Earth.
- He looks exactly like (insert movie star, cartoon character, brand logo, etc.), except different.

I hear that sort of statement from independent contracts all the time. With Annie, there were times when I'd have to ask her to be more specific, and there were times when she had to trust my judgment as an artist.

I think what really solidified our working relationship is that we both went into it cautiously, but with high hopes. We were respectful of one another and were willing to give something that could've been awful for both of us a try.

Thankfully, it turned out to be one of the best decisions either of us ever made. That does not mean that we didn't have our share of difficulties getting started, however.

The first cover I ever worked on for her was the cover for *Murder with My Darling*, and the first draft of that cover was laughably terrible. I mean just bad.

This was no reflection on Annie's authoring skills or my abilities as a designer, but rather, it was a reflection on our learning to trust each other enough to be honest. Annie was afraid of scaring me away, and I was afraid of letting her down. The result was that neither of us was willing to speak our minds about the project until it had come together in the most God-awful conglomeration imaginable.

Annie and I still burst into laughter, when we remember this first trial run of ours, because it led to something beautiful. It led to trust.

We figured out that by being willing to give and take, to communicate our ideas and doubts even if they went against the original plan, we were able to create a masterpiece that continues to catch attention to this day. Later that year, I created the cover for *Chocolate Can Kill* that reached a sales ranking of #12 on the Barnes and Noble website.

Despite that rough start in 2012, Annie shocked me by asking if I would become the exclusive cover artist for Annie Acorn Publishing. This meant that I would be handling not only her covers, but the covers for every author who was published through her company. It was an astounding offer, which I gladly accepted.

In addition, a few weeks later during a business call with Annie, I mentioned that I had written poetry in my earlier years. She shocked me again, when she asked to see a sample of my writing.

I remember being entirely too embarrassed to send her anything that I had written in my younger days and found a more recent bit of fan fiction I had written about a favorite show of mine. I remember shaking my head as I sent it to her, unwilling to believe that I had just sent an award-winning author and major publisher a piece of fangirl fiction.

I adamantly denied being good enough to write professionally. After all, being the cover artist for the company was already a dream come true. Less than twenty-four hours later, Annie offered not only to publish me, but to actually contract stories from me. Needless to say, 2012 was a good year for me.

In the spring of 2013, I was asked to attend an informal gathering of women authors published under Annie's banner. In addition, she requested that I be the guest speaker and give a small demonstration of what I did as a cover artist, complete with a little show-and-tell type pamphlet.

I took this task with extreme trepidation, as anyone who knows me will tell you that I'm not very good with public speaking, and I envisioned a massive crowd of successful women staring up at me as I tried to explain how Photoshop layers resemble an onion.

Also, I was pretty sure that I was about to lose all credibility as their go-to cover designer. After all, I didn't have a great professional portfolio or a great public speaking background on which to fall.

Having just turned 25, I didn't consider myself the seasoned professional these women were surely expecting.

Plus, this would be the first time Annie and I would meet in person.

Obviously, my fears were unfounded. During that meeting I made great friends with those authors and further solidified Annie's respect for my position in her company. She was so impressed with the presentation I put together, that it ultimately formed the idea in her mind for the very book you're now reading – an outcome I still have trouble believing.

In the end, the most I can tell you is this:

While I was a complete greenhorn in the realm of professional cover design, un-seasoned and un-prepared for the greatest step towards an actual professional career I've made to date, everything worked out.

I believe it worked out because:

A) It was orchestrated by a Higher Power, and
B) Annie and I took our failings and successes in stride.

Annie has always been willing to listen to my side of things, and I to hers. We are both willing to give and take, even if it means that our 'big vision' gets put on the back burner, because we understand that it's not about stroking our individual egos, it's about attaining a mutual goal.

If an artist and a writer, who had never met before in their entire lives and could not have been any more different individually if they'd tried, can pull something like that off, then there's hope for anyone who is still searching for that kind of professional partnership.

Authors vs. Graphic Cover Designers

The argument can be made that authors and graphic cover designers are more alike than different.

- Both are creative beings, who are ultimately geared towards selling a product – a book.
- Both must have a clear idea of the content of the story being told.
- Both benefit from clear, efficient, effective communication and mutual respect.
- Both gain from a thorough understanding of who represents the potential buyer of the book, for which a cover is being designed.
- Both seek a pleasant, productive, successful relationship.

Annie Acorn and Angel Nichols

Understanding the Importance of Illustration

Angel Nichols –

The Importance of Cover Art:

Have you ever wondered why you put so much effort into your work, and yet, it doesn't get the attention it deserves?

Art is a versatile topic, and there is no Golden Rule, where art is concerned.

However, if we're talking about marketing, then you must remember that first impressions are quite often last impressions.

Most of us know the old saying *Don't judge a book by its cover* – one of the most popular colloquialisms in history for a reason. It is human nature to make judgments based on appearances.

Here's the ugly truth: Unless you sell a whole lot of books in Braille, 99.9% of your client base will choose to purchase or pass on your book based on the cover art.

If the cover art is sloppy, buyers will assume that the writing is sloppy. If the cover is dark and depressing, they will assume that your story is dark and depressing. By the same token, if the cover art is clean and bright, they will assume that what it covers is the same.

You should take as much care planning and designing the cover illustration as you do on the story itself, because the cover will ultimately sell the book. So, now that we have established the importance of your cover art, let's discuss how great cover art is produced.

Composition:

Before your cover art can tell your story, it has to be created. In order to create such work, one must first know and understand the basics of great illustration – Balance, Symmetry, and Color.

Balance –

Balance refers to how your images are placed or composed within the space of the cover. The concept of balance can also apply to the color scheme or even the choice of typeface used for the book's title.

You absolutely want a perfectly balanced illustration.

Balance is NOT the same as symmetry, referring more to the overall feel of the picture.

Is it too heavy or too light? Is there too much empty space at the top, the bottom, or in the middle? Do the colors match, or do they match too much? Is the focus where it should be, or is the image too crowded to have any focus at all?

All of these questions refer to the balance of the image.

Symmetry –

Unlike balance, which is essential to a great cover design, symmetry is a question of artistic interpretation and is not, therefore, necessarily something that you want.

As human beings, we respond favorably to perfect symmetry.

Did you know that we automatically consider the two halves of each person's face to be symmetrical when, in fact, less than 6% of the population has perfectly symmetrical features? Why is that?

Simply put, we translate symmetry into beauty.

If you want your buyers to feel cozy or at peace, a symmetrical design may be the very thing that inspires those feelings.

Personally, as a designer, I find symmetry to be overrated. Still, it can be important to making or breaking a design.

This is the point at which graphic design leaves science and becomes art, and where a top-rate graphic designer shines above the rest.

Another important consideration is the interplay between symmetry and asymmetry.

A symmetrical design does not have to mean that one side mirrors the other. It can mean that you have a tall object on both the right and left sides of the image. It could also mean that equal amounts of accent color appear on both sides of the image.

One of the most memorable things I learned in art school was that empty spaces can be just as important as the ones filled with objects and text.

Asymmetry can call even more attention to your cover than symmetry. Symmetry is beauty, but asymmetry is uniqueness.

Creating an asymmetrical design can be a strategic decision, based on what kind of reaction you want to get from your potential buyers.

Do you want them to be a bit disturbed by the image? Do you want them to feel that something's not quite right?

This could be the deciding factor as to whether or not they feel your story will be worth their time. Particularly if your book falls within the categories of mystery, thriller, suspense, or horror, asymmetry can be the very thing that pulls potential readers in.

Color –

Color is possibly THE most important decision your illustrator will make.

Placement is key, but color is connected to our emotions. One study showed that wall color could directly influence how an individual does on a test, regardless of subject.

People tested in green rooms felt calm and focused. People in blue rooms felt calm, sleepy, or even depressed. People in orange or red rooms felt aggressive and unfocused, and people in yellow rooms felt, believe it or not, hungry.

Think of the color white.

What do you feel? What images come to mind?

White is a sterile color – clean and safe. Clouds, feathers, and illumination all come to mind.

And then, there's black. What do you feel, when you think about black? Darkness, fear or, perhaps, a little sexy?

Black is the absence of color, the opposite of its counterpart. It conjures up images of dungeons, little black dresses, and creatures of the night.

Just from this demonstration, you can see that color affects your potential buyers more than the images presented themselves.

Color is a broad subject, but you should have a basic knowledge of how it works, if you are to understand the process of graphic design and be able to communicate well with an illustrator.

We've all seen a color wheel at one point or another, right? Colors that complement, and colors that contrast.

Think about the mood you want to set in your image.

Is it a peaceful feeling? Go with greens, blues, and pinks.

If you want something a little more lively, then yellows, oranges, reds, purples, or even a splash of bright blue should do the trick.

The colors you and your graphic designer choose will set the mood for the entire story.

If it's whimsical, purples, whites, blues, and pinks are your territory. If it's a fiery romance, blacks, dark purples, reds, and oranges are your desired palette.

The wrong color can give the wrong feeling, which could send a potential buyer walking in the other direction.

Typography:

What's in a name? A lot, actually.

People consistently and constantly overlook the importance of typography, the use of text as art.

Your book's title isn't just a title. Your title is part of the cover art, just as much as the color scheme or the background you choose.

Do not underestimate the value of a fitting typeface. Color, depth, style, placement, and size are all factors to consider when designing your title text.

An eye-catching title can save an otherwise boring design, and it can also be the very thing that allows your design to be overlooked.

Too many authors get stuck on fonts such as Times New Roman and Arial. Typefaces are whole different animals these days.

There are typefaces that crumble, shatter, and shock. There are creepy fonts, romantic fonts, bold fonts, ancient fonts, and fonts that look as though aliens created them.

Common misconceptions surrounding titles include:

- The words all have to be the same font.
- The words all have to be the same size.

- You can't use fancy fonts in titles, because they're too hard to read.
- The way the title looks should come last on your To Do List.

Overall Impact:

The keyword in Cover Art is ART.

Each cover should be just as much of a masterpiece as the pages that appear inside. Cover art should never be rushed, pieced together, or random.

Your cover art should reflect the most captivating part of your story, before the reader ever picks up the book.

Art has many rules and, ultimately, none at all. In theory, art is expression.

The difference between the art that hangs in the Louvre and the art on the cover of your book is that your cover art doesn't just tell **your** story or express **your** feelings. Cover art should relate more to your potential readers and buyers than it does to you.

Keep these things in mind, but also remember that it is OKAY to break some rules once in a while. Sometimes, it will be the crazy thing that puts you on top.

Communication:

This is THE MOST IMPORTANT element of a fantastic design.

For those of you who contract out your illustrations, these things may seem more like something your contracted designer should consider, and for the most part, you would be right. However, it is just as important for you to understand these basic principles, because not everyone who claims to be an artist is a great illustrator.

Other than in the case of Annie Acorn and AAPub, the most annoying thing my clients have done in the past is to NOT communicate with me.

An illustrator's job is to take your vision and turn it into a reality. Illustrations are an extension of your storytelling. If your illustrator has an unclear picture of what you want, then the illustration will be unclear.

In addition, having at your fingertips this basic knowledge of composition, balance, symmetry, color, typography, and the importance they play in designing an illustration will enable you to speak your graphic designer's language much better.

The more you and your illustrator communicate, the more you will be on the same page. As you work together over time, a good graphic designer will develop the ability to remain one step ahead of you, as they become more familiar with your writing style and you learn even more about their illustration techniques.

Nothing is more frustrating than to be paired with an incompatible business partner, and this goes for authors, publishers, and illustrators alike.

Ultimately, the author or publisher should have the final say on what they do or don't like, but it is their illustrator's job to give them the best possible options from which to choose. By understanding the basics of what illustration is all about, you will be better prepared to know what you should expect to see as the design develops.

Your illustrator should have artistic freedom throughout the process, but you as the author or publisher should be very clear about the mood you want to set, the overall impact you want it to have, and the elements within the design that are a must.

For instance, if you are writing a romance novel and all you tell your illustrator is that you want it to be a romantic scene, that leaves a lot of room for interpretation.

Do you want it dark? Dreamy? Steamy? What do the characters look like? Is it inside or outside? Is it nighttime or daytime? Is it a date? A stroll through the park?

These details will help your illustrator understand what the scene is, and then it becomes their job to turn it into an eye-catching, buyer-drawing design.

In Summary:

- First impressions are last impressions.
- It is human nature to make judgments based on appearances.
- Buyers purchase or pass based on cover art.
- The three basics of illustration: Balance, Symmetry, and Color.
- Balance refers to the overall feel of a picture.
- Symmetry is a question of artistic interpretation.
- Symmetry isn't always desirable.
- Humans translate symmetry into beauty.
- Empty spaces can be as important as objects and/or text.
- Symmetry is beauty, but asymmetry is uniqueness.
- Color is possibly THE most important decision made.
- Placement is key, but color connects to our emotions.
- Your book's title is part of the cover art.
- Try and mix different fonts and sizes.
- The keyword in the term Cover Art is ART.
- Cover art should reflect the most captivating part of the story.
- Art has many rules, and ultimately, none at all.

- Cover art should relate more to potential buyers than to you.
- It's OKAY to break some rules once in a while.
- Sometimes, it will be the crazy thing that puts you on top.
- Communication is THE MOST IMPORTANT element of a fantastic design.
- Not everyone, who claims to be an artist, is a great illustrator.
- The most annoying clients fail to communicate with their designer.
- Understanding the basics will help **you** to communicate.

My Aunt Grace

Both of us have spent part of our lives in the Deep South, a region that's noted for folksy, but common sense sayings. One of them that pertains to working with a graphic designer goes like this:

If you wouldn't say it in front of Aunt Grace, then don't say it!

In other words, if you can't say something with grace and decorum, then it's probably best if it remains unsaid.

In case you haven't picked up at least a hint of this yet, then we'll state it more plainly now – COMMUNICATION is one of the major keys to forming a successful, professional relationship.

Enough said…

Angel Nichols and Annie Acorn

A Peek Behind the Scenes

Annie Acorn –

When I was a little girl, living in Columbus, Ohio, I used to eavesdrop on party-line phone conversations, when I was supposed to be napping. I learned all sorts of things as a result of my vicarious listening until one day, due to my total innocence, I shared a bit of juicy gossip I had overheard with my mother. Needless to say, the room where I took my naps changed from that day forward.

Over the past several years, Angel and I have exchanged many emails as part of our working relationship, all of which have contributed in some shape, form, or fashion to our successful, ongoing relationship.

Then, as I was listing some of the topics we might want to cover in this book, it dawned on me that it might help those of you, who are interested in building a similar partnership, to see some of the actual communications that have occurred between us.

The first email thread that popped into my mind was the one surrounding the cover for *Cramped Quarters – Mary's Trunk* by Ron Shaw, the first ebook to be published in a series AAPub handles for Ron.

Now, the Whale, as we all know him, is a fairly astute kind of guy, and yet, when I read him the instructions I had sent Angel for his initial cover, he was astounded, both by the input I contributed to the process and the degree of detail I offered.

For this reason, I hope some of you, at least, will find our email exchange useful as you work to increase your understanding of the cover design process. So, here goes:

Me to Angel:

Angel –
This is to confirm that the first of the Cramped Quarters covers is the thing we need for you to be working on now. The title should read:

Cramped Quarters
Mary's Trunk

All the covers in this series will have the title Cramped Quarters with the second line changing. For this cover I want a camel-backed, also known as a humped-back, trunk in golden brown leather with gold or brass fittings to be front and center. A warm spotlight of some sort should be illuminating it from above. If you pull up several and want my opinion, I'll be glad to give it.

On this cover, the trunk will be closed. On successive ones, it will slowly open. The author's name is Ron Shaw.

Behind the trunk, acting as a neutral background, I want us to see two side walls and the back wall of a dusty, somewhat haphazardly arranged antique's store - very subdued and muted - almost like an old sepia photo that's faded. Think that it should appear almost as if it's a faded wallpaper in the background, so that the viewer's eye will only really see it if they look for it.

The trunk MUST be front and center and might even appear slightly oversized. It might be nice if it were sitting on some sort of oval rug - just thinking aloud here. We also discussed that I would like the walls to appear as if they're leaning slightly inward at the very top, giving an unusual perspective, since this series is about a ghost.

You'll know best about the Fonts for the title lines, etc., but certainly a clearer, Gothic type font would be in order if you can find one that a viewer can still readily read.

This series is aimed at women readers and has a romantic element, although it is primarily a ghost story. For this reason, I would suggest any reds you use should be a darker red as opposed to a bright blood red that would lend itself to horror.

Also, a version of this cover will eventually be seen in both the larger print size and the postage stamp size we see on websites for the ebooks.

Please let me know when you have an estimated time of completion for this one. I think the next assignment coming your way will be the cover for the *Annie Acorn's 2015 Valentine Day Treasury*, but that could change.

Have a great day!
Annie

Angel's reply to me:

Alright, this is what I've come up with. Let me know if you want the other size, or if you want me to change something.

I'll go ahead and say that the trunk appears to be slightly off center because the wall in the background is off-center left and the table in the foreground on the right is further in than the table on the left, creating the illusion that the chest is just slightly further to the right than it actually is.

I don't think it's a problem, but let me know if it bothers the author or yourself, and I can attempt to change it.

My response to Angel:

Angel –
Overall, I like it. We're definitely on the right track.

Two things:
1. Is there any way that you can soften the corner on the lighter area behind the words Mary's Trunk. The sharp rectangle strikes me as a bit out of place.
2. I'm a little concerned that, as busy as this cover is, the black letters of Cramped Quarters won't show up well in the postage stamp size, even with the gold/yellow borders. Is there any other color we could try that would go well with the rest of the cover? Maybe even a rose red? Thoughts?

I'm finishing the edits on Susan Jean Ricci's *A Valentine's Day to Remember* for the treasury with her in a few minutes, and I think that's the cover I'll have you do next. Have you had any ideas re the cover for the actual treasury yet? How's your Valentine's Day story coming along? Peggy is finishing hers up as well.
Thanks,
Annie

Angel's return to me:

Okay, a couple of different things.
One of these has the main title in a lighter gold color and the block behind the sub-title stretches the width of the cover.
The second one has a bit more done to it. The title is rose-colored with a light gold border that is about 10 points thicker. The glow is a light rose, the sub title is also much lighter with a rose border and a blurred box behind it that is also a lighter rose color.
I did a few things to the top of the chest to make it less stark than the previous covers. Let me know what elements you like from each, or if you prefer one over the other.

My reply to Angel:

We have a WINNER! The rose.jpg one is perfect. I do like the less stark treatment on the top of the trunk as well.

Can you send me this second cover in both sizes attached to the same email?

I'm going to send you the instructions for Susan Jean Ricci's cover by separate email, so that we start a new gmail chain for it.

So, did you learn anything as you 'listened in' to Angel's and my emails? A couple of things struck me as I read back through them:

- I started out by clearly defining my ideas and expectations.
- I requested an estimated time of delivery for a first draft.
- Angel explained an oddity to me right away.
- I let her know both what I liked and suggestions I had.
- She offered me choices, obviously understanding my concerns.
- I kept her advised of other work coming her way soon.

This next exchange is about the cover of the book you are now reading and is much briefer.

Me to Angel:

Also, we're obviously going to need a cover that will work well in both large and small sizes. Since I'm doing the project management, so to speak, I thought I'd leave that part up to you - the expert. :-)

One way we could go, since the Annie Acorn brand does draw, would be to use my ATOW figure, showing her painting a cover on a large easel. On the other hand, you could also do something really graphic.

Honestly, I'm looking forward to seeing what you come up with, especially since By Annie Acorn and Angel Nichols will take up a fair amount of space. :-(

Now, my suggestions made sense from a business standpoint. We would've saved time and money by incorporating existing artwork, and brand recognition is a draw.

Still, as you will see, Angel felt perfectly comfortable and wasted no words, as she utilized her reply to quickly put me in my place, her knowledge and expertise lifting our view of the cover to a higher level.

Angel to me:

As for the cover design itself, the simpler the better. We want the title to stand out on this, so that readers immediately understand that this is not a design manual for illustrators.

I'll throw some suggestions your way, once I have some ideas, but cartoons might not be the best way to go for this one, as cartoons paired with the word 'design' often gives the impression of a 'how to draw' book, which could potentially scare away anyone who thinks they don't have artistic ability.

I'm thinking something along the lines of what we did with *The Young Executive* with an illustrator on one side and an author on the other, but without the line down the middle. It needs some thought, but that's where my mind is headed currently. What do you think of that?

As you can see, once Angel had made her position clear, she still requested my input – a nod to our mutual respect for one another and the collaborative nature of our relationship.

One of the things I've learned from working on book covers with a graphic designer is that neither of us ever really knows what to expect. Case in point, the cover for Susan Jean Ricci's *A Valentine's Day to Remember* – a cover both Angel and I thought would be a breeze.

Since the story revolves around houses, I suggested that Angel begin with the snow-covered house we had used for the cover of my own *Too Busy for Christmas*, removing the snow and adding some Valentine's Day decorations on the evergreen tree and the front door, as well as in the windows.

Angel complied, doing exactly what I had requested, and the result was **horrible**. Stripped of its snow covering, the house lost all of its cozy appeal, turning into a plain, box-like structure.

Also, the green grass that now took up much of the cover created an overall impression of summer, completely inappropriate for a February holiday. In addition, the bottom third of the cover was virtually empty except for plain driveway. Neither of us was very happy.

I suggested that Angel add some residual snow to the roof, change the trim colors on the house from a stark white to creams, brown the grass as if it were Bermuda grass in the winter, float some fluffy clouds in the bright blue sky, and add a dog and ball pulled from the story to the driveway for color and action – not bad ideas, coming from a small town gal with no training.

Being a trooper, my stalwart graphic designer once again came through, although the cover was still lacking. A good cover has to draw a potential buyer's eye, and this one was no more exciting than a drive through a cookie-cutter subdivision.

Still believing that we were on the right track, I suggested that Angel line both sides of the driveway with hearts on sticks and enlarge the hearts on the tree's garland.

At this point, my talented collaborator took things in hand. Instead of two rows of single hearts on sticks along the driveway, she placed one row of taller, multi-colored stacks of hearts on sticks along one side of the drive, thereby better maintaining the balance of the piece.

Then, she did, as far as I was concerned, the most extraordinary thing. She took the stark blue sky with a few fluffy clouds, stratified the clouds, and overlayed the entire thing with a pink and rose sunset – AMAZING!

Presented with the cover for her story, Susan Jean Ricci was ecstatic, and I let out a sign of relief, as I once again thanked God for leading me to Angel Nichols' bio as a result of my web search.

Susan and I both agree that the cover for her *A Valentine's Day to Remember* is now one of our all time favorites. THIS, folks, is how and where your graphic designer earns their keep.

Sometimes, though, it isn't the cover that's the problem. Sometimes, if you're acting as a go-between on a cover design for an author or group of authors, it's the writer or writers themselves who are the problem.

In this situation, I had been completely blindsided by the author's initial reaction to a cover that Angel and I both agreed fulfilled its role perfectly. As emails flew back and forth, this particular author's language grew harsher, and I could tell that Angel was losing patience, as revision after revision was completed.

Stuck in the middle, I focused on dodging bullets, finally coming to the sad conclusion that, if we couldn't resolve the situation in an amicable manner soon, I would be forced to tell the author that AAPub would be withdrawing from her project.

The alternative would have been to lose Angel, and not being an idiot, that was a complete non-starter as far as I was concerned.

The following is an email I sent to Angel in an attempt to move things forward in a more positive way, after she had presented me with a completely different cover, based on her own ideas after having read the entire book herself in an attempt to gain insights into what might work best.

Not only does it show how we handled the situation as a team, but it also includes some examples of how I've learned to curtail my own reactions to various designs.

From me to Angel:

I've pointed out during my conversations with her that she really is expecting the impossible, as neither you nor I are capable of reading her mind, and therefore, we are never going to completely duplicate her vision of what a cover should look like.

I've also stressed that you are a highly trained, very talented artist who is also a writer, which gives you a unique understanding of each story. This one really resonated with her when she saw your new cover. I've also taken some time to discuss with her the fact that it is often a shock for me as well, when I first see your designs.

For instance, when we were upgrading the covers I had initially done in Gimp, I sent you the black and red base image I had used for my two mortgage books. When you sent me the .jpgs, I thought I'd be opening a black and red cover, and instead I opened silver and green - much lighter and much less dramatic.

My initial reaction was that I didn't like them, but then I closed your email and did something else for a few minutes, so I could come back to the covers without my preconceived notions of what to expect.

Bingo! Suddenly, they looked quite nice on my screen, and since I've uploaded them sales have been substantially better. Kudos to you for recognizing that the lighter, more modern looking cover would appeal to a broader audience.

Another one that was somewhat of a shock was the cover for *Travels with Little Annie*.

I had asked for and had even drawn for you, when we were in Birmingham together, a two dimensional road with things along it, almost like a children's board game. Instead I got a straight line road coming right at me, and again I stepped back.

I also made myself look closely at each individual thing that you had used because I was seeing some things that I really did like. Finally, I realized that, once I had gotten over that initial shock, it was the color of the car and Annie's eyes as well as the Statue of Liberty that were bothering me.

The first two were pretty easy fixes, but I never could express to you what was wrong with the statue. It wasn't until you exchanged the chunky S of L with the see-through Seattle Needle that I realized it was too solid an object in what was a really full cover. This one is now one of my favorites among the covers you've done for us!

I think my having to step back sometimes is akin to your changing the track changes on the story I had edited for you from red to blue, because in your mind it made the criticisms seem less harsh.

I can't tell you how much our working relationship means to me. You allow me to have input and make tweaks without getting all ego, and I hope you know how much I respect your talent and expertise and value and rely on your input.

Sometimes my tweaks work and sometimes they don't, but it makes me feel more comfortable to at least have seen them.

Often, you do exactly what I've asked you to do, and the result is horrible. Occasionally, you like the change, and I don't. Ultimately, it's a matter of taste.
Annie

Soooo…

I asked Angel what she thought of these examples, and she responded that she was struck by our ability to communicate electronically without allowing anger to enter into our discussions.

Bottom line, we're professionals, and because of our ongoing respect for each other, our relationship has deepened in time to one of friendship.

Email can feel impersonal, but the person receiving your message still has feelings. One way to avoid improper emotions entering into your collaborative relationship is to stick to the facts when corresponding electronically.

Also, as I've noted before, Angel and I are both careful to leave the door open for comments and ideas from the other.

Treating the person you are emailing in the same manner as you would wish to be treated yourself will always lead to a better result. Grandma was right. Good manners will never fail you.

Paying for a Cover

Why should I spend money on a cover?

Your content is unique. You've spent months, sometimes years on your project. A generic cover won't reflect the special qualities of YOUR story.

Ultimately, the financial success of your book may very well reside within the quality of its cover.

How much will it cost you, if your book doesn't sell? In money? In embarrassment? In heartbreak?

Contracting with a graphic designer to produce your book's cover, may well be the best money you'll ever spend.

Annie Acorn and Angel Nichols

Speaking Your Illustrators Language

When I was a little girl, my father was in the U.S. Army and our family was transferred to Germany for a tour of three years. We would later complete two more tours in Germany for a total of nine years.

The first year, I was afraid to go anywhere off base, because of a single simple thing – culture shock. I remember especially how difficult it was to communicate with anyone, because I couldn't understand what people were saying.

Later, I realized this fear was ridiculous, and it probably kept me from enjoying my life in Europe as much as I did for the rest of our stay. At the time, it was very real to me, though.

This is an example of the most common language barrier scenario, but the fact is that it plagues everyone at some time or another, even if they never set foot outside their own country.

America, specifically, is so diverse that the language barrier can occur between you and your own neighbors, even if they speak perfect English. This is never more evident than when a mathematician explains the Pythagorean theorem to anyone who barely passed fifth grade math or when an artist explains color theory to an author.

Our own talents can get in the way of proper communication and can leave each of us alienated in our own homes. The way we overcome this social hurdle is the same anywhere in the world. You have to learn to speak each others' languages.

Thankfully, speaking 'artist' is infinitely easier than learning to speak German. Hopefully, the outcome will be the same, and you'll have less fear, when attempting to connect with a professional artist.

Here are some tips:

1. Illustrators are visual people.

We see things in our minds, even during regular conversation. We see things in great detail, which is what makes us good at what we do.

Usually, so are authors. When you write a scene, you think about how things look, taste, smell, sound, and feel. So do artists.

The difference is that we know which colors convey what emotion and how to set a scene to draw your eye to a specific point on the page. So, when you're describing what you want on your cover, don't worry about giving us the back story, we just want the details for how you want the scene to feel to the reader. Use emotion to describe the scene.

2. Use a lot of adjectives to describe the scene.

Is it fiery and dark? Is it feathery and light? Is it intense and dramatic? We can choose the colors and lighting that fit these emotions.

3. Don't try to paint us a picture.

That's our job. Keep an open mind about what colors you want, because you might find that your dark green theme doesn't work too well in your candy shop scene. Let us find the colors and the balance, but if you really want something specific to come through, don't be afraid to let us know, we'll find a way to incorporate it.

4. Trust your artist.

We know what we're doing, and chances are that we might really surprise you at how well we interpret your thoughts into a visual image.

That being said, don't be vague when telling your artist what you want. We're great at interpreting thoughts into images, but we're not psychic. Tell us what you want, and then let us do our thing.

5. Don't be afraid to ask for changes!

Yes, artists can be picky, touchy people. It's in our nature. However, if you've chosen a professional, they'll be more than happy to adjust your image to suit your needs. It is, after all, your cover, so don't settle for something that you don't like.

However, don't be surprised if your artist gets a little miffed at you if you decide to completely scrap your original idea and go with something completely different mid-project. The reason is usually not money or time related, but rather that artists tend to be single-task people. We need to finish a design once it's started.

Have you ever had a scene that you absolutely had to finish writing, even if it was four o'clock in the morning, because if you didn't your head would explode? It's like that.

6. Sometimes, artistic terms are complete gibberish to anyone who isn't an artist.

We aren't trying to make you feel stupid. We're using our own language, and sometimes we forget that most people don't have a clue what cel-shading is or what blending modes are.

Here's a quick list of common terms to familiarize yourself with:

Hue: The tone of a color.
Saturation: The vividness of a color. The more de-saturated a color is, the more grey it is.
Value: The lightness or darkness of a color.
Color Number: All digital colors have a hexadecimal (comprised of a combined total of six letters, numbers, or both) number that an artist can put into their photo editing software color palette.
　　If you want a specific color, look that color up on the internet and find its number. There are a few sites that can help with that, one of them is http://www.mikesclark.com/web_management/html_colors.html.
RGB: Stands for Red, Green, Blue. RGB color mode is best for images that will remain on the internet.
CMYK: Stands for Cyan, Magenta, Yellow, Black. This color mode is best for images that will be printed, because printers and printing software use CMYK colors exclusively.
Layers: Most photo editing software is comprised of layers that the artist can draw on and turn on or off, so that you can see them individually or together. Think of them as if they were pieces of transparent paper all lying on top of one another.
Pixels: Pixels are tiny squares that make up every single digital image you've ever seen.

Canvas sizes in photo editing software are usually made up of a pixel number, which determines how many pixels and, thus, how much detail an artist can work with.

Generally speaking, anything that is 72 pixels per inch (ppi or dpi for printers) is low resolution, and anything 300ppi is high resolution.

Canvas: Even digital artists use canvases. It's the area within which we create your image.

Shading and Light: These terms refer to the shadows and light sources in the image.

Keep in mind that light often comes from two different places, and that it bounces off solid objects.

If your artist says something about light that you don't understand, ask them what they mean. They should be able to explain it. If they can't explain it, I suggest you get a different artist.

Tablet: The digital artist's tool is called a tablet. It functions like a pressure pad that the artist draws on. The pressure of the 'pen' is translated into marks in the artist's software.

If your artist uses a term with which you're not familiar, ask them to explain it.

7. Be patient.

Getting to know another person is never easy, especially when it's a working relationship that is often relegated to the phone or internet.

If your artist's work is not satisfactory, don't stop communication and leave them in the wind. Talk to them and ask what they need in order to see the scene more clearly.

It may help to send your illustrator the paragraph or chapter from which the scene is taken, as it will enable them to understand the context. Feel free to send them links to sample images that you've found that are similar to what you want. They can use them as inspiration.

8. Ask for an estimate in advance.

Art takes time, and unfortunately, it's an extremely undervalued practice.

Be sure to ask your artist to provide you with an estimate for each project. Additionally, ask them to let you know if they're going to go over their estimated hours.

Sticker shock is not fun for either party, but neither should you expect quality art for free. Be sure to pay your artist what they ask for.

If you think the price is too steep, ask them about it. They may be willing to give you a discount.

9. If your image isn't what you want, but you just don't know why, ask your artist what they think about it.

It's possible that you've requested a color scheme or a specific setup that doesn't work well visually. Your artist will do as you ask, but they might know what's bothering you about the image better than you do, and may be able to offer suggestions on how to fix it.

10. Finally, if your artist just isn't working out, don't string them along.

We like to know that our art is appreciated and that our time is not being wasted.

Pay your artist the appropriate amount for any work that has already been done, and then politely tell them that you've decided to go in another direction with your project and that you won't be needing their services any longer.

Be careful that you aren't violating any agreement, written or oral, that you've made with your artist prior to letting them go.

Artists are a tight knit community, so try not to burn any bridges. It's possible that your reputation will proceed you when you look for other artists.

Also, most of us don't mind working together, so if you think adding a second artist to your project will help, consult your artist about it. You might be surprised at what a little cooperation will achieve.

How Late Is Too Late?

It is never too late to call in a graphic designer to illustrate your book's cover – period.

At whatever point in the publication process your relationship begins, make sure that your illustrator has a clear understanding of the content of your story and your vision for its cover.

If you don't have a clear vision, communicate this to your graphic designer immediately. A true professional will be happy to guide you through the process, so that they can provide you with a book cover that both satisfies you and provides your book with the best chance to attract buyers and achieve financial success.

If you need help or need to change designers, don't hesitate.

Angel Nichols and Annie Acorn

Questions and Answers

Q: How do you come up with your ideas?

Angel:

When it comes to writing stories, it helps to have a publisher who contracts a story from you, haha.

If Annie just says, "Write me a Christmas story.", then yeah, I have to go through a process. The first thing I have to decide is what genre I want the story to be in, because I write in multiple genres.

Once that's settled, it's a matter of coming up with a baseline idea. For instance, *The Ghost of Christmas Present* started out as the idea of a haunted mansion. That's it. From there, I start writing and developing characters, asking myself who, what, when, where, why, and how.

As for illustrating, it starts out pretty similarly. The author usually has a general concept, and if not, I ask them what the most intense or most important scene in the book is. Images develop from there, as I try to strike the right balance between aesthetics, practicality, and efficient use of space.

On the other hand, my hobby art is a totally different animal, which usually starts out as a mess and ends up as a different mess.

Annie:

Let me start out by saying that I don't believe Angel Nichols has ever created a mess with her art in her life.

Ideas for my writing generally come from one of three sources – an experience, a character who takes up a position in my mind and won't budge, or a strong sense of a particular place. My *A Christmas Rescue* would be an example of the former, *A Clue for Adrianna* that I wrote as Charlotte Kent epitomizes the second, and my entire Luna Lake Cabins series, especially *Love's Third Chance,* represents the third.

Coming up with a vision for a book's cover design is, for me, similar to the process I utilize to write the book's blurb. Basically, I ask myself what would most capture a potential reader's attention and make them want to purchase the book.

Sometimes, it's a quote. Other times, it's a signature prop that shows up throughout the story – for instance, the chocolates that appear on the cover of *Chocolate Can Kill.*

Q: Did you ever have any doubts about working with each other?

Angel:

Oh, absolutely. I wasn't entirely sure that Annie was sane when she called me. No offense, Annie.

I mean, there I was, fresh out of college, not a single professional piece to my name, and here's this award-winning author in charge of her own publishing company calling me up based on what I wrote in an artist's bio almost a year earlier.

Not only that, later I found out that she had narrowed it down to six artists, of which I was the youngest and most inexperienced by FAR, and she had asked Andre, another associate of AAPub, to blindly choose one, just to see if he would pick me from the lineup as well, which he did. So, yeah, I had my doubts.

Four years later, and I still can't believe we've been as successful as we've been. Everything you'll ever read about working relationships will say that our story shouldn't have worked.

Annie's an experienced professional woman, who lives in the northern part of the U.S., and I was a fresh-faced nobody, who lived a thousand miles away with nothing but some drawings I'd done for friends and a story about my father drawing a mouse in purple crayon.

She was nuts to trust me with the future of her company, but she did, and it totally worked out for both of us.

Annie:

Okay, I admit to being nuttier than a fruitcake, but have you ever heard the expression **crazy like a fox?**

Anyone who has ever owned a company will tell you that being an entrepreneur of a start-up business is basically the same as jumping from a high diving board without knowing for sure whether or not there's any water in the pool towards which you're headed.

Sure, Angel was young. Sure, she was inexperienced, but on the flip side, this might possibly have meant that she would be more willing to listen to my needs and wants than someone older and more experienced, who thought they knew what I wanted and needed more than I did.

Also, despite what Angel says, the artwork displayed on her website was **amazing**!

At the end of the day, neither Andre nor I cared if she had done millions of covers. What if she had created millions of *bad* covers? What we cared about was that she had talent, and that was screaming at us from her illustrations.

I never doubted that things would work out, once we'd passed the first five minutes of that initial phone conversation. Angel was polite, professional, willing, and available. I'd already seen that she was talented with my own eyes.

Now, it was just a matter of our learning to trust and respect one another, and I believed we were both the sort of people, who would make that kind of commitment to any relationship we believed in.

Q: How have your past experiences influenced your respective abilities?

Angel:

Well, that's one thing that Annie and I have in common. We share a similar history, and without going into a lot of detail, we were forced to become independent women sooner than we should have been.

My family was a military family, so we moved a lot, and while that experience gave me a deep appreciation for different cultures, it was also very isolating. I found my strength in expressing myself through drawings at a very young age, and I also had a deep and incredibly strong relationship with God.

Those things have given me an ability to write from multiple perspectives and to understand how people think. My mother jokes all the time that I should've been a lawyer, and my husband says I could've been police chief by now with my investigative sense. That certainly helps when I'm trying to translate ideas into images.

Annie:

I am on record as saying that, while some are born with a silver spoon in their mouth, I was born holding a pencil and pad of paper, one in each of my hands. I learned to read very early, and words have flowed through my mind ever since.

Still, it is my varied experiences that have provided the locations, scenarios, and characters for my stories. Couple that with a love of playing with words, and you have yourself a writer.

Also, there was a period during my college years, when I seriously considered becoming a graphic designer. Circumstances intervened, and I ultimately chose a much different path. Now, though, I enjoy working with Angel and watching each book cover come alive – a little bit of that past dream coming true.

Q: The saying goes *write what you know*. Is that solid advice?

Angel:

I think so, but there's something to be said for trying new things, too. If you want your character to be a pilot, but you've never been a pilot before, that's okay as long as you do the proper amount of research in order to create a believable character. If someone who's a pilot in real life can read your story and say, "That's accurate.", then you've done a great job, even if you've never set foot in a cockpit.

Annie:

Definitely! Almost every time an author, who's work I've been editing, has gotten into trouble, it's been because they've written something about which they either had no knowledge whatsoever or had done incomplete research.

Cases in point – horses and weapons.

If you've never ridden a horse and don't understand the concept of how many hands tall a horse is, then you're in danger of placing a 6'4" man atop a Shetland pony. It's also essential that you understand the difference between English and Western terminology, for instance bridle vs. reins.

If you've never hunted or done sport shooting, then you had better seek the knowledge and advice of an expert, when you're determining the type of weapon and damage caused for the murder mystery you're writing.

The same is true when you're working with a cover designer. Sometimes, I've known exactly what I've wanted, as when I assigned Angel the cover for *Cramped Quarters – Mary's Trunk* in the email example above. On the other hand, after my first feeble missive, I turned the design of this nonfiction book's cover completely over to the graphic designer in her.

Q: Do you find it difficult working together long-distance?

Angel:

I know it's a challenge for Annie sometimes, because I'm often at my part time job or unable to answer the phone. I try to keep my replies as close to less than 24 hours later as possible, but sometimes there's a bit of a lag.

Otherwise, email is my BFF. It helps me keep things in order and lets Annie send me a complex list of details that I can refer to at a later time.

So far, I've never missed a deadline, knock on wood.

Annie:

Simple answer? At times, yes!
I find it frustrating that, while I'm a writer by nature, there are some cover ideas I would prefer to sketch for Angel.

What I wouldn't have given on a few occasions to be able to sit down with mugs of tea and create a cover with her, something we've managed to do a couple of times over the years when we met in Birmingham.

Also, I prefer to describe verbally what I want because it's quicker, while Angel prefers a written assignment.

Most of the time, I allow her to win this battle by sending an email assignment, but there are some covers, particularly those where I'm in some doubt as to what I really want and want to discuss these issues with her in an effort to save time and trouble, where I request a phone conversation, understanding that I will be paying for her time here as well.

Q: Can you articulate how you both interact to other types of working relationships?

Angel:

Sure, absolutely. Any working relationship, even romantic relationships, come down to mutual respect, trust, and communication.

If you can maintain a civil tone with each other, treat each other as you would want to be treated, hold up your end of the deal, and remember to communicate honestly and politely, then it'll work.

Also, it helps to have a mutual obsession with your craft and a love of chocolate.

Annie:

DITTO!

Having said that, it helps if the other individual is a genuinely nice person and the chocolate comes in the form of Lindt milk chocolate truffles.

Q: Be honest, have you ever had a major disagreement?

Angel:

Not that I can recall. In fact, the closest we've come was probably a project that Annie mentions elsewhere in this book, where another author just could not make up her mind about how she wanted her cover to look.

It cost Annie a great deal of money and me a great deal of time, but I don't actually recall either of us getting upset with the other during that incident. It was more of a third party frustration.

Annie:

Never, but then, it's hard to have even a minor disagreement with someone who is genuinely doing their best, remains calm, remembers their manners, and knows how to listen.

Q: Annie, you publish a variety of stories from other authors as well as yourself, and Angel, you write and design the covers for all of these stories as well as working independently. How do you both manage to have time for all that?

Angel:

Haha...good question. Uh, well...

I have to attribute that to coffee, hot tea with LOTS of sugar, and massive amounts of determination. Otherwise, it comes down to common sense and time management skills.

If you have to get up earlier in the day or DVR your favorite program for later, then do it. It also helps to get the proper amount of rest and to have a nagging desire to finish what you begin.

Annie:

LOL! I don't have the time to do it, which makes the fact that somehow it all seems to get done even more of a miracle.

One thing that helps is that I'm very goal oriented, so I don't tend to waste a lot of time on things that aren't really important to me. Also, I'm a list person, and I learned a long time ago how to best prioritize my lists, as well as how to divide and conquer the items that appeared on them.

Pitchers of espresso and bowls filled with chocolate candies help, too!

Q: Was the cost of what you do ever a problem?

Angel:

Actually, yeah, it was at first, but not in the manner that you might think.

I recall Annie actually scolding me for my hourly prices being *too low*. It took her almost a year to convince me to raise my prices, but I did.

As I've matured, I've come to realize that I got really lucky with Annie, because there are a lot of people who would've taken advantage of that naiveté without a second thought.

Annie:

Only with my conscience during that first year, but I was working on the problem.

One thing I've always appreciated is that Angel understands the limitations with which I'm dealing as the owner of a start-up company.

On the other hand, I try to maintain a steady level of work from AAPub in Angel's InBox, so that she can have some idea of what sort of income she can count on from us. For instance, I may have her do the cover for this year's *Annie Acorn's Christmas Treasury* in January, simply because I have nothing else to assign her and I know the need will eventually come.

Q: Do you have any advice for someone struggling with writing, publishing, or designing?

Angel:

- Find your own way.
- Don't be afraid to ask for help.
- Realize that there are more resources at your disposal than you think.
- Be bold, and
- Trust God.

Timidity is charming, but it won't get you anywhere professionally, and neither will acting like a jerk. Just be a nice person, continue to practice what you do, LEARN TO TAKE CRITICISM, and hang in there. It'll all work out.

Annie:

All of the above, plus:

- Observe what makes those you admire successful.
- Concentrate on learning your craft.
- Try, try, and try again.
- Learn how to review your own efforts honestly.
- Practice time management.

In my own case, taking the road not traveled, answering the beat of a different drummer, and not only thinking outside the box, but often acting as if there was no box have been critical components in some of my most successful endeavors.

Good luck!

Incorporating Graphic Design

While your graphic designer's primary purpose is to produce your book's cover, they also bring with them the expertise that allows for expansion of your book's presence in social media and website environments.

For instance, Twitter is arguably the best venue through which to market your baby.

Often, authors choose to open a Twitter account that they will use strictly for tweeting events about or quotes from their book. A small avatar of the book's cover or a distinguishing feature from the cover, such as the trunk used for *Cramped Quarters – Mary's Trunk*, could make or break the success of such an account.

Also, don't forget to attach to your tweet that gorgeous cover your graphic designer worked so hard to produce!

Prefer to tweet only as the book's author? Then a sparkling, anime avatar might be a positive when attracting new followers.

Be sure and request such avatars in several sizes, so they will work well in all sorts of website environments, including guest posts on other bloggers' sites that can form important additions to your overall marketing plan.

A good graphic designer will have done this all before. All you have to do is raise your hand and ask the question.

Annie Acorn and Angel Nichols

Illustrating Your Own Book Cover

Ten Dos and Don'ts

Being both an educated illustrator and a published indie author gives me a unique point of view when discussing this particular topic. I can see both sides of the coin, and I have a sympathetic understanding for each perspective. Believe me, they can be very different at times.

As creative minds, both illustrators and authors see the world through different lenses than most other people, and we tend to be passionate about our respective crafts, sometimes to the point of overlooking the importance of each other.

While I understand and support educated artists and feel strongly that, if you can employ an artist for your cover you should, I also know that sometimes cost is prohibitive. Sometimes you just don't want to involve a second party.

Some of that has to do with common communication problems between authors and illustrators, which I've addressed elsewhere in this book.

For now, let's look at some of the pitfalls you should avoid if you absolutely must create your own cover art.

1. Words are Art Too!

As an author, you should understand this more than most. Words are powerful, they shape governments and topple kingdoms (at least, in our books they do!), and so it shouldn't be any surprise that they can absolutely ruin your cover as well.

The title, sub-title, and author tag are the first words that anyone will ever read on or about your book. The tricky part is getting them to blend with your cover art without being lost in it. You want the title to stand out and be seen, but you don't want it to completely overtake your artwork either.

There are literally thousands upon thousands of completely free fonts all over the internet that are super easy to download and use. They come in everything from 'Disco' to 'Romantic' to 'Old-School' feels.

This resource is extremely useful, but be careful not to cross the line with outlandish or overdone fonts. Here are a few examples of what to look for and what to avoid:

A) The typeface you use should convey the theme of your book. If it's a romance, choose something romantic. If it's educational, pick something that is neat and easy to read. Don't immediately settle for Times New Roman, and NEVER use Comic Sans for ANYTHING.

B) Don't go overboard with effects and colors. Don't be afraid to color your title, but make sure that the colors don't clash with your background. If you don't understand the difference between clashing colors and contrasting colors, take a look at point number 2 on this list.

C) Use photo editing software to your advantage. Most programs like Photoshop come with some useful tools specifically for fonts. This includes kerning control, size control, and some useful layer effects to make your title glow or have a unique outline. Experiment with these effects and learn what they do.

2. Colors, Colors, Everywhere.

Color is in the top three of this top-ten list for a reason. It is possibly the most misused and misunderstood element of any amateur and, sometimes, of professional design work.

Color can get you into SO much trouble, and it can also be the deciding factor on whether or not your design sells your book. Let's be honest. What's the first thing people see when they look for a book? It's the cover, and thus, the cover art.

Your writing may be stellar, it may rival Shakespeare, but if your cover doesn't convey that visually to the shopper, they will never pick it up to find out. This is where an artist's education comes into play, as we've been instructed on the proper use of color and the dynamics of color.

Most people understand what primary (red, blue, yellow) and secondary (green, purple, orange) colors are; however, when dealing with digital color, there's much, much more to consider.

Here are some basic things to remember and avoid:

A) Observe your surroundings. Nothing is ever just a solid color.

There's always light that makes colors bounce off each other. Gradients, for example, can be a lifesaver when trying to add depth to a background.

Notice that the sky is never a solid color of blue, but rather it tends to get darker the closer it is to the horizon and lighter towards the sun. The sun is another good example, it's never just yellow, but rather has a white center and gets progressively darker towards its edge, sometimes getting into the maroon and purple colors during sunset.

B) Understand the differences between contrast and clash, complimentary and monochromatic colors.

Contrasting colors are colors that are opposites. For instance, green and red are opposites on the color wheel, which means that most shades of red (maroon red, fire-engine red, apple red) as well as red's adjoining colors on the color wheel (orange and yellow hues) will also contrast with most shades of green.

Clashing colors are contrasting colors that are so intense they're fighting for attention. This has more to do with saturation (the intensity or vividness of the color) than the actual hue.

Complimentary colors are colors that are often paired together in order to enhance them both. For instance, purple and green are often paired, because they are not exact opposites of each other, but they are far enough apart on the color wheel to create some interest.

Monochrome or monochromatic colors are colors that are different shades of the same hue. For example emerald green and grass green would be two different colors, but of the same hue and, therefore, monochrome.

C) Never ever use solid black or solid white for shadows and highlights. This seems like an odd rule, but it's probably the one that most amateur artists trip over.

Shadows are never solid black and highlights are never solid white. The world is made up of different colors that bounce off each other and reflect onto other surfaces.

If you set a white cup on your table and just look at it for a few minutes, you'll start to see that there are other colors being reflected onto its surface. Your shade of skin, the table, the walls, even the color of the ceiling will have an influence on the color of the mug.

Instead, go for deep unsaturated colors for shadows, and use very light unsaturated colors for highlights. Use highlights sparingly. The most saturated or intense colors should be in between, and you should never use a color at 100% saturation. That's neon territory, and nobody wants to look at that.

3. The Devil's in the Details.

Try to keep a single event or scene in mind when doing your cover. This is a tough one for author's to understand, because you try to convey as much detail and sensation in your writing as you possibly can.

Trying to put everything from your book onto your cover will only crowd it up and make it confusing. The cover of your book is not the place to make a collage of all your favorite parts of your story.

Instead, pick a scene that communicates to your readers what the overall theme of the book is. If it's a romance novel, pick a romantic scene.

Remember that mystery is part of what makes people want to look closer, so you don't have to show everything in the scene. Sometimes just a single item can convey a sense of what the book is about. Half-eaten chocolates on a pillow, a necklace on a satin sheet, that sort of thing.

Other times, you might want to show the reader a window into the world inside the book, such as a cliff overlooking the ocean at sunset. Whatever it is, you can add detail, but just make sure that it's not so much detail that the viewer doesn't understand what you're trying to say.

4. Use Resources.

There are so many useful tools and websites on the internet that it's a little overwhelming. If you have a problem, ten times out of ten, someone else has already had that problem and has written a blog about it.

You can find tutorials on anything, resources for free fonts and paintbrushes, stock photos of most subjects, and websites that create color palettes for you. There are even sites where you can ask artists advice about your image and get feedback for free.

There is literally no end to the amount of help and information you can find, so USE IT. Just be sure that you use it properly, pay the correct fees (if there are any), and don't fall into the very easy trap of stealing by slightly altering other peoples' work just because it's easier. Artists don't make as much money as you might think, so leave their creations to them and make some of your own instead.

5. Back Up and Re-Invent!

Always make sure to save copies of your work for future reference, and don't be afraid to redo it over and over again until you like it.

Also, I've learned this the hard way, *always* keep a backup of your stuff on an external thumb drive or cloud drive. This is in case your program or (God forbid) your computer crashes on you.

The thing about digital art is that it's so easy to just erase and do over. You can create a new layer and keep the old stuff for later if you want to. Don't be intimidated by your photo editing software. Use it to your advantage, as long as you save your files and back them up, you can do whatever you want with it.

6. Sometimes, Simple is Better.

This goes back to point number 3. Sometimes, too many details are just too much. When in doubt, keep it simple. If you can't tell what's going on in the image, chances are your readers can't either.

7. Check You Resolution.

This is very important, because it affects how you see colors on your screen.

Make sure your computer screen is set to the correct resolution and color settings before you begin creating your cover. If you create something, send it for a second opinion, and your viewer says that the colors look weird, it's possible that your monitor color settings aren't correct.

Check with your user manual for your computer, or go online to get instructions on how to change and check those settings.

8. Avoid using untouched photos as backgrounds.

This goes double for online books that only have electronic covers, because their viewing size tends to be about as big as a postage stamp.

Untouched or unaltered photos do NOT scan well and will look muddy or grainy. If you know how to alter a photo with photo-editing software, then do so. Otherwise, avoid using photos as backgrounds.

That does not mean that you can't use a photo as inspiration. Chances are there's a stock photo with good lighting and contrast that's very similar to your photo.

9. Size matters.

At least with covers it does. Be sure that you know what size image your printer or online host needs before you create your cover. This is for two reasons:

First – It saves time in the long run.
Second - If you create an image that's drastically larger or smaller than what you need, your image may become blurry in its real size, or your image might be cut off in

some parts on its printed counterpart. It would be a shame to spend so much time on something that people can't see clearly.

10. Don' t Stress.

This is something we creative personalities really need to work on.

The more you stress over your cover, the image, the money it would take to get a professional illustrator, etc., the less creating you're actually doing.

We illustrators sometimes develop tunnel vision. We'll spend hours trying to perfect a single detail on an image, before we realize that the image as a whole is going nowhere.

In order to avoid this, take a step back. Literally, lean back or walk away and look at your image from a distance.

Take a break, go for a walk, drink some tea – whatever it takes to calm your nerves and stop the stress from destroying your cover.

Never settle for something that was rushed or something that you don't 100% love. It's not worth it to have your hard work represented by something that's less than what you want it to be.

That being said, perfection is overrated. Art is fluid, and sometimes it will take you places you didn't even know were possible.

Set your general guideline for what you want, and then let your imagination take over.

Little Touches

Little touches can go a long way. For instance, one of us always insists that the other one exchange tiny holly berries and leaves for the dots over "i's" on Christmas book covers. Can you guess which one of us that is?

On the other hand, one of us definitely prefers that authors' names appear front and center on a book's cover.

Tiny things, perhaps, but they can both send strong subliminal messages.

Angel Nichols and Annie Acorn

Cost of Cover Design

In this day and age, the cost of book cover designs ranges from the free, generic cover templates available on most sales vendors' websites to thousands of dollars for a professionally designed cover and everywhere in between.

Unfortunately, paying more does not always mean an author or publisher will receive more, and as with most things, this is a buyer beware market.

If a designer sounds too good to be true, promising an award-winning cover every time, or consistently pushes too hard against your wishes, then it would probably be in your best interest to cut your losses and move on.

As with any major purchase, the wise buyer searches widely and seeks references from those who have utilized a particular designer's services.

Ask questions, such as:

- How approachable was the illustrator?
- How easy was it to reach them by phone or internet?
- How responsive were they to author or publisher input?
- Did they meet deadlines as requested?
- Did they provide what the previous user considered to be a quality, professional cover that appropriately supported the marketing of their book?
- Was the designer willing to negotiate price?

We all have to start somewhere, and a beginning illustrator, who's feeling their way, may be extremely talented and even vastly experienced in other artistic arenas. Such designers may be more willing to work within your budget.

Keep in mind that, if you are publishing as a boutique publisher or indie author, your book and its cover could remain available for many years or even decades. Consequently, the ultimate cost of a bad cover could become astronomical.

Annie Acorn and Angel Nichols

Resources

Color Help:

Paletton.com is a great website that is equipped to help you pick from every known digital color in the world, and it will even automatically choose for you complimentary, contrasting, and monochromatic colors.

Stock Images and Models:

DA Stock (http://www.deviantart.com/browse/all/resources/stockart/) is a webpage with stock art from different artists of varying talent. Not all of this stock is free, but most of them just require artist credit for use.
Concept Art Stash (https://www.pinterest.com/conceptartstash/) is a Pinterest page devoted to quality stock from models to textures. This page contains professional nude models among other things.

Custom Brushes for Photoshop:

Brusheezy.com is a nice little website with many free custom brushes for Photoshop, from bubbles to flames.
MyPhotoshopBrushes.com is another great site with free custom brushes and textures.
PhotoshopFreeBrushes.com is also a great site for, what else? Free Photoshop brushes.

Free Fonts:

Dafont.com has many professionally created specialty fonts.
1001fonts.com is another great site for free fonts and typefaces.

Help and Advice:

Lynda.com (http://www.lynda.com/) is a website devoted to teaching you new skills and how to develop your talents in almost any category you can think of.

OTHER TITLES AVAILABLE
FROM
ANNIE ACORN PUBLISHING LLC

By Annie Acorn

Chocolate Can Kill
Murder With My Darling
Luna Lake Cabins – The First Year
Love Heals (Coming Soon!)
The Magic Sand Dollar
A Tired Older Woman: Loses Weight and Keeps It Off!
Cover Design and YOU!
Pen & Ink 2014

Annie Acorn writing as Charlotte Kent

A Clue for Adrianna
A Man for Susan
Love's Journey
Love's Surprise
One Sweet Christmas
A Magic Cup of Christmas Tea
A Christmas Kiss
A Valentine Surprise

By Angel Nichols

Cover Design and YOU!
The Ghost of Christmas Present and Other Stories

__Christmas in the Mojave__
__Christmas Love Exchange__
__Jolly Old Spook__

By Susan Jean Ricci

__My Sexy Chef__
__Dinosaurs and Cherry Stems__

By Peggy Teel writing as denise hays

__Niki Knows the Dirt – A Niki Edgar Mystery__
__Monkey Business – A Niki Edgar Mystery__

By Peggy Teel

__God and Grandma__

By Juliette Hill

__Pink Lemonade Diary__
__Finding Christmas Love__

By Billie Thomas

__Murder on the First Day of Christmas__

Angel Nichols

Angel Nichols is an accomplished illustrator, author and graphic artist who juggles a busy working schedule with family, friends and her passion for the arts. She has been a hobbyist writer for much of her life, before being asked to author for *Annie Acorn's 2012 Christmas Treasury* in which her short story, *Christmas in the Mojave*, appears. Her *Christmas Love Exchange* is included in *Annie Acorn's 2013 Christmas Treasury*, and her *Jolly Old Spook* graces the pages of *Annie Acorn's 2014 Christmas Treasury*.

Ms. Nichols' *The Ghost of Christmas Present and Other Stories* has thrilled an international audience, and Annie Acorn Publishing LLC was honored to be able to include her *A Rose by Any Other Name* in the *Annie Acorn's 2015 Valentine's Day Treasury*. She is a member of From Women's Pens.

Ms. Nichols is the exclusive cover artist for Annie Acorn Publishing LLC. Her award-winning covers have been seen on the Barnes and Noble's bestseller list, as well as in Amazon top categories. She has a Bachelor of Arts in Visual Communication and Digital Design from AIU.

You can follow her at @Angel_Nichols.

Annie Acorn

Annie Acorn is the pseudonym of a prolific, internationally beloved author, whose readership recognizes her mainly for her women's fiction, cozy mysteries and richly woven stories with a warm southern flair, such as Chocolate Can Kill and her Luna Lake Cabins romantic women's fiction series. She writes her romantic women's fiction/family saga Captain's Point Stories series as Charlotte Kent. She is a founding member of From Women's Pens – A Cooperative of Women Writers.

Annie is the mother of two sons. She lives in the Washington, D.C. area, where she has done extensive technical writing as a contractor.

She owned a tri-state medical outsourcing business for a number of years and was the Director of a behavioral healthcare firm. She once flipped a comic book and collectible retail company comprised of five stores, and she has managed cemeteries and funeral homes. She is the owner of Annie Acorn Publishing, LLC.

Ms. Acorn has published in The Inspirational Writer, and she edited an in-house publication for the State of Mississippi. She is a contributor of ezine articles.

In her spare time, Ms. Acorn enjoys reading, writing mysteries and romantic women's fiction, listening to classical music, playing cards, and spending time with her family and friends – often at a restaurant serving delicious food.

Annie is the author of the blog at annieacorn.com. You can friend her on Facebook and tweet her at

@Annie_Acorn. She will respond to your email sent to annieacorn11@gmail.com, and she invites you to visit her AAPub author's pages at:

http://annieacornpublishing.com/authors/annie-acorn and http://annieacornpublishing.com/authors/charlotte-kent.